Gfile

Make this *G file* your own! At the back you'll find some stickers. Write your name on the 'name' sticker and stick it on the outside – now you'll never lose it!

Published by Girlguiding UK
17-19 Buckingham Palace Road
London SW1W 0PT
Email: chq@girlguiding.org.uk
Website: www.girlguiding.org.uk
© The Guide Association 2005
Reprinted 2006

Girlguiding UK is an operating name of The Guide Association.
Registered charity number 306016. Incorporated by Royal Charter.

ISBN 0 85260 165 4
Girlguiding UK Trading Service order code: 6628

Printed by Sterling Colour Print

Project Editor: Alison Griffiths
Designer: Angie Daniel
Illustrator: Katie Mac
Photography by: Laura Ashman, with additional photography by
Henry Iddon, John Mills, Dave Henderson
Writing group: Sue Bell (Guide Adviser), Gillian Ainsley,
Maud Cunningham, Catherine Holgate, Jenny Stevenson, Liz Taylor
Project Coordinator: Verity Hancock, Chris Ridley

Girlguiding UK would like to thank the Guides and their Leaders
who took part in the development and testing of this resource.

Users are reminded that during the lifespan of this publication
there may be changes to:

🧩 Girlguiding UK's policy

🧩 legal requirements

🧩 practice by governing bodies
which will affect the accuracy of the information contained within
these pages.

Although the terms 'parent' and 'daughter' are used in this resource,
users should remember that what is said may apply to a guardian or
other adult with parental responsibility, or their ward.

Contents

Themefile:

My name is

I joined Guides on

I was/was not **a Rainbow in the**

unit.

I was/was not **a Brownie in the**

Pack.

My favourite things

Colour

Pop group/star

Food

Drink

Animal

Hobby

Book

School subject

Best friend

Sport

I am a member of

_____ Guide unit.

We meet at (place)

_____

On:
Monday	
Tuesday	
Wednesday	
Thursday	
Friday	
Saturday	

at (colour in time)

88:88

Our subs are

_____

Our Leaders and helpers are:

_____

Paid:
Weekly	
Monthly	
Termly	
Yearly	

We have

_____ Patrols.

They are:

_____

5

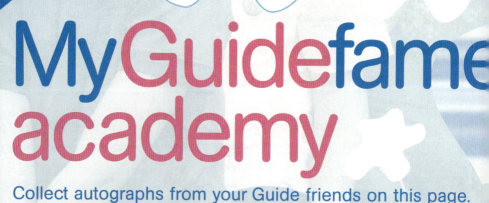

My Guide fame academy

Collect autographs from your Guide friends on this page.

A girl's guide to Guides

What is Guides all about? Well, think of... fun, friends, excitement, going away, helping people out, travel, new experiences, having a say and making a difference... and you'll get the idea!

Being a Guide means being a team player. You're a member of a Patrol, a unit, and also the largest female voluntary organisation in the world. You'll make friends all over the place, try things you have never even thought of doing, and basically have a really good laugh!

The fun starts here!

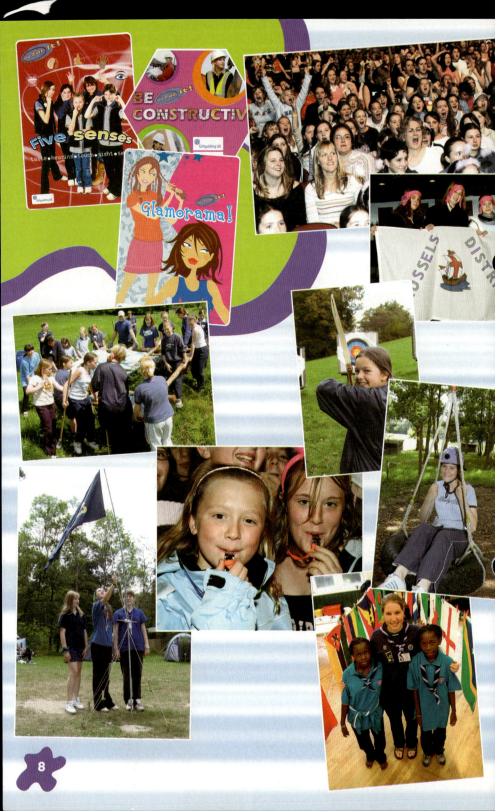

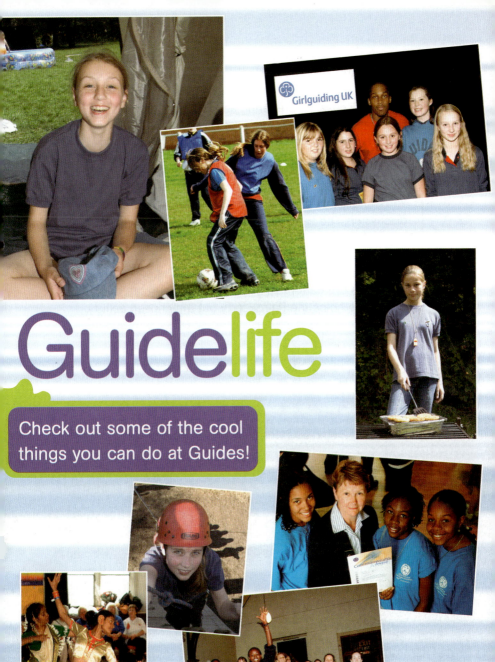

Guidelife

Check out some of the cool things you can do at Guides!

At Guides, you'll be a member of a Patrol: a team of four to eight girls who spend a lot of time planning and doing things together. You'll share in discussing, preparing and enjoying activities – but most of all, your Patrol will be great mates who you'll have fun with!

You'll choose a Patrol Leader (PL) by a secret vote or a Patrol discussion. The PL is your team leader, and she'll pick a Patrol Second (PS) to take over when she's not there. When your Patrol gets together to talk about things, like which Go For It! or activity to choose, the PL listens to everyone's ideas and helps the Patrol make its mind up. When the decision is made, she helps the Patrol carry out the chosen activity.

Patrols

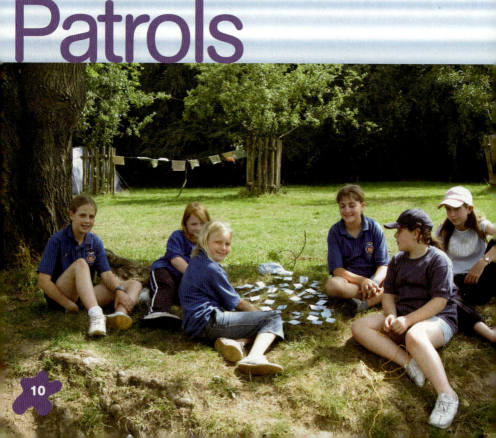

Sometimes there are decisions to be made for your unit, like where you want to camp or ideas for Community Action or outings. Then the PL represents her Patrol at the Patrol Leaders' Council. This is a meeting of all the Patrol Leaders, Leaders and Young Leaders in the unit. Your PL will talk to the whole Patrol first and then take your ideas to the Council.

No two Patrols are alike, because they are all made up of individuals. Patrols can change as new Guides join, Guides leave, or the members decide it's time for a change. Patrol Leaders can be elected from other Patrols and Patrol Leaders can choose their Seconds from other Patrols.

Patrol names

- Caterpillar
- Daffodil
- Daisy
- Dolphin
- Eiffel Tower
- Elephant
- Lion
- Panda
- Parrot
- Pelican
- Penguin
- Poppy
- Puffin
- Pyramid
- Rose
- Shamrock
- Sphinx
- Starfish
- Taj Mahal
- Thistle

Every Patrol needs a name. Patrols can choose their own name from this list, or make up a name to reflect the interests, hobbies and personalities of the Patrol members. Badges are available for the Patrol names listed here. If you choose your own name you could make your own badges.

ThePatrolLeader

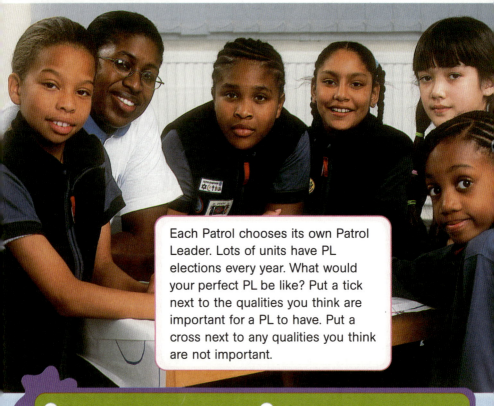

Each Patrol chooses its own Patrol Leader. Lots of units have PL elections every year. What would your perfect PL be like? Put a tick next to the qualities you think are important for a PL to have. Put a cross next to any qualities you think are not important.

- Friendly
- Kind
- Good at everything
- Organised
- Thoughtful
- Caring and sharing
- Oldest Guide in the Patrol
- Full of good ideas
- Bossy
- Keen
- Good example
- Enthusiastic
- Your best friend
- Has been in Guides longest
- Most popular Guide
- Loudest Guide

Each Patrol Leader is different; she'll be good at some things and not so good at others.

What qualities do you have? Fill in the three best things about yourself.

Is there a quality you could improve on?

If you are a caring, sharing, enthusiastic team member, you will help your Patrol to work together. This helps your PL to lead the team.

Give yourself a sticker if you become a PL!

ThePatrolSecond

The PL chooses her Patrol Second. She should pick someone she can get on well with and who the rest of the Patrol will like and respect.

Give yourself a sticker if you become a PS!

Patroltime

Patrol Time is time to spend together as a team, doing all the activities you have planned. Some units have a short period of Patrol Time during every meeting, while others may have one full meeting a month or term.

The most important thing is to have fun and enjoy being a team.

Patrols can do loads of fun things together: play games, make things, work for badges, make up songs and dances, learn new skills, do quizzes, cook, help others – the only limit is your imagination. You can choose to work together on Go For Its! – see page 34 for more info.

Sometimes activities will go well, and sometimes they won't. It doesn't matter – you don't have to be perfect! Just try to use what you've learned from your achievements and your mistakes, to make future Patrol activities more successful.

Check out *Patrol x-tra* for more Patrol fun ideas!

To show that you belong to Guides, there are lots of different things you can wear. You can choose from this range of tops. What you wear on the bottom half is up to you. Maybe you'll want to wear shorts in hot weather, and jeans or casual trousers in winter.

To see all the Guide wear, ask your Leader if you can borrow a copy of the guiding catalogue, or take a look at **www.girlguiding.org.uk/shop** .

Guidewear

A gilet is a great idea – it keeps you warm and you can sew your badges on it too!

Your Unit Guidelines are a set of ground rules written jointly by the Guides, Leaders and Young Leaders in the unit. They are designed to keep everyone safe and happy at Guides. Examples of Guidelines might be:

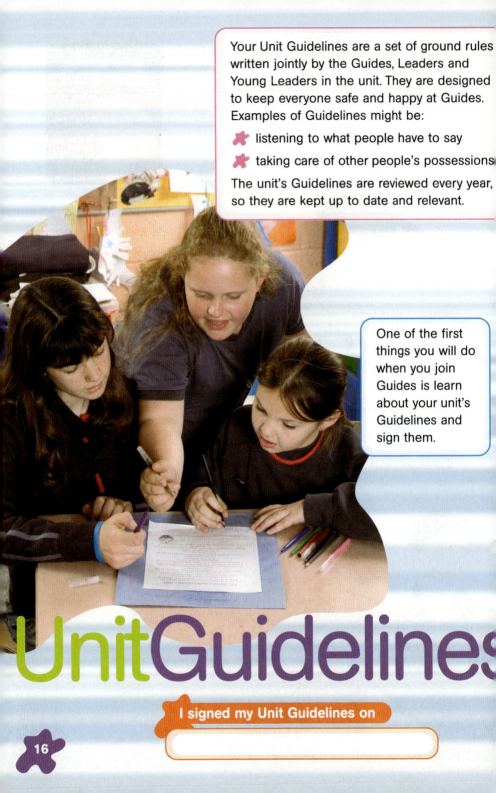

- listening to what people have to say
- taking care of other people's possessions

The unit's Guidelines are reviewed every year, so they are kept up to date and relevant.

One of the first things you will do when you join Guides is learn about your unit's Guidelines and sign them.

UnitGuidelines

I signed my Unit Guidelines on

The Guide meeting

At your first meetings, you won't only be getting to know your Patrol and signing the Unit Guidelines. You'll also be discovering a lot more about how Guides works. Your unit might have routines that they follow every week, like paying subs, giving out information, or ending the meeting.

The Guide song, Taps, is often sung at the end of the meeting:

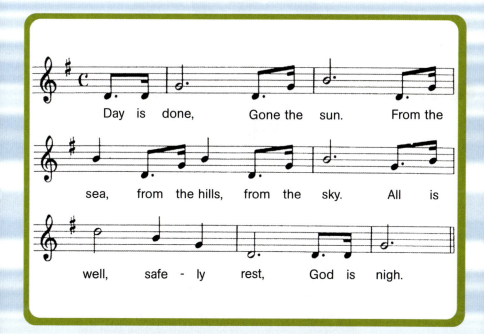

Day is done, Gone the sun. From the sea, from the hills, from the sky. All is well, safe - ly rest, God is nigh.

No two meetings will be the same, because the activities will always be changing. Remember, it's you and your Patrol that will help make the choices about what goes on.

Promiseanc

What is the Promise all about
and why do we make it?

The Promise...

... is the common link between all Girlguiding UK members – even the youngest members make the Promise!

... represents the spirit and ideals of guiding.

... shows your commitment.

... is individual to you.

... makes Guides different to other youth groups.

I promise that I will do my best:
To love my God,
To serve the Queen and my country,
To help other people
and
To keep the Guide Law.

Law

The Guide Promise is not just some words to say – it is something to think about and act on in daily life. It links you to Guides all over the world, who all make a similar Promise.

I promise that I will do my best

Promising means taking on responsibility to do or not to do something. Everyone has different interests, skills and abilities, but if you accept the challenge and try, you will be doing your best.

To love my God

Belief in one's God is very personal. No-one expects you to know everything about your God, but you are promising to learn more about your faith and what it means to you.

To serve the Queen and my country, To help other people

This includes respect for people, animals and the environment, and being a responsible citizen. Being helpful all the time isn't as easy as it sounds!

And to keep the Guide Law

Adopting the Laws as guidelines will help you 'live the Promise' and develop your own beliefs and values.

KeepingthePromise

How can you 'love your God' if you live your life without ever considering what that means in the real world? How can you serve the Queen without ever meeting her? Does the Promise only apply when you're wearing Guide uniform, or does it matter in every aspect of life? Talk to a Guide who has already made her Promise, and look at these pages for more ideas.

Loving your God

Give yourself a sticker when you:

* do something helpful out of doors
* help out a friend or family member
* think about the special things in your life.

Serving the Queen and your country

Give yourself a sticker when you:

* work on a community project
* learn about your history and culture
* do a 'Good Turn'.

KeepingtheGuideLaw

The Guide Law is a set of rules which Guides try to keep all the time, not just at Guide meetings.

Guide Law

A Guide is honest, reliable and can be trusted.

A Guide is helpful and uses her time and abilities wisely.

A Guide faces challenge and learns from her experiences.

A Guide is a good friend and a sister to all Guides.

A Guide is polite and considerate.

A Guide respects all living things and takes care of the world around her.

Think of different ways to keep these laws, and give yourself a sticker each time you achieve one.

You choose when you are ready to make your Promise. You can also choose how you would like to make it. Making your Promise will be a really special ceremony that you can look back on – a 'mountain-top moment'. Talk to your Patrol about where they all made their Promises, or look through these ideas to get you started:

Makingyour Promise

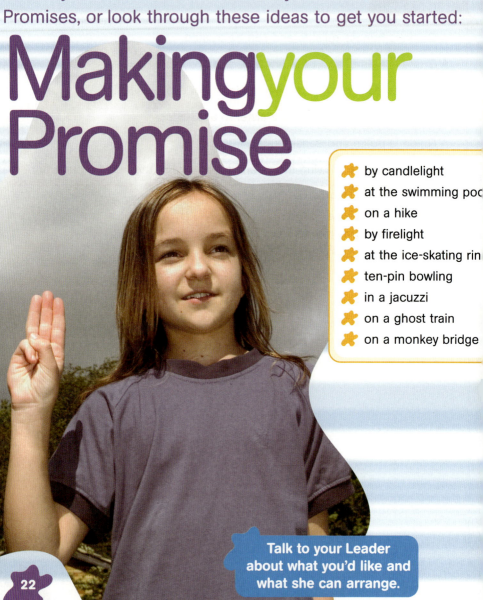

- by candlelight
- at the swimming poo
- on a hike
- by firelight
- at the ice-skating rin
- ten-pin bowling
- in a jacuzzi
- on a ghost train
- on a monkey bridge

Talk to your Leader about what you'd like and what she can arrange.

22

Mountain-top moments

Your Promise ceremony is your real 'mountain-top moment' – so write the details in the flag on top of the mountain!

There will be lots of other things you do as a Guide which are really special or memorable. Record them in the clouds.

Guiding

A brief history of Guides...

| 1908 | 1910 | 1912 | 1914 | 1916 | 1920 |

1908
Robert Baden-Powell, the founder of Guiding and Scouting, published *Scouting for Boys*, which led to the start of Scouts.

1910
Guides began because girls wanted to do the exciting things that Scouts were doing.

1912
Lord Robert Baden-Powell married Olave Soames. The first *Guide Handbook* was published.

1914
Brownies started.

1916
Rangers began for those girls getting too old for Guides.

1920
Lord Bad Powell wa made Wc Chief Scc

WorldThinkingDay

Lord Robert and Lady Olave Baden-Powell had their birthdays on the same day – 22 February. Since 1926, this has been a day for celebrating Guiding and thinking about Guides and Scouts around the world. For this reason it is called World Thinking Day.

24

imeline

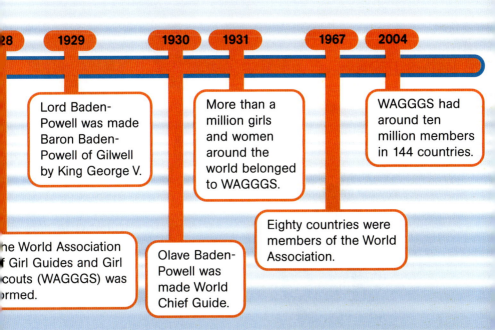

28   **1929**   **1930**   **1931**   **1967**   **2004**

Lord Baden-Powell was made Baron Baden-Powell of Gilwell by King George V.

More than a million girls and women around the world belonged to WAGGGS.

WAGGGS had around ten million members in 144 countries.

Eighty countries were members of the World Association.

he World Association f Girl Guides and Girl couts (WAGGGS) was ormed.

Olave Baden-Powell was made World Chief Guide.

In your unit you could celebrate World Thinking Day in different ways. Some units raise money for the World Thinking Day Fund. This is a special fund of money which helps more girls become Guides all round the world, including in the UK. Check out the WAGGGS website **www.wagggsworld.org** to find out more.

However you choose to celebrate World Thinking Day, there are girls like you doing similar things all around the world.

25

Who: Rainbows

Age: 5–7

Do: Rainbows Look, Learn, Laugh, Love – and have lots of fun!

As a Guide you can become a Rainbow Helper, which means you go along and give a hand at Rainbow unit meetings. You get this badge to wear on your uniform.

Guiding

Guides are just one part of a wider guiding family. Find out how Guides fit into the guiding family in the UK. Check out the members' pages at **www.girlguiding.org.uk** for more info.

Who: Brownies

Age: 7–10

Do: The Brownie Adventure includes all kinds of fun, games and activities!

If you would like to help at a Brownie unit, ask your Leader about becoming a Pack Leader. If you were a Brownie, you need to have been in Guides for a year before you can be a Pack Leader.

Who: Guides

Age: 10–14

Do: Everyone knows that Guides are...

Groovy,
Ultimately
Independent and
Definitely
Extraordinary
Superstars!

amily

Who: Senior Section

Age: 14–25

Do: Everything – from Community Action to travelling the world! Turn to page 107 to find out more!

Who: Adults

Age: 18+

Do: Leaders (Guiders, Assistant Guiders and Unit Helpers) are the adults responsible for running your Guide unit. However, there are lots of other adults who might help you while you're a Guide. For example, the person responsible for all the Leaders in your area is called the District Commissioner – you'll need to talk to her if you take your Baden-Powell Challenge (see pages 71–92).

IntheUK...

Districts = all the units in your area

Divisions = all the Districts in your area, town or city (not every area has Divisions)

Counties = all the Divisions in your County (like the county that you live in, but a large county may have many guiding Counties)

Countries or Regions = all the Counties in your area of the UK. Girlguiding UK has six Regions in England (Anglia, London and South East, Midlands, North East, North West, South West) and three Countries: Cymru/Wales, Scotland and Ulster.

Where do you fit in? Mark your town, village or city on the map.

Find out what District, Division, County and Country/Region your Guide unit i

District

Division

County

Country/Region

Scotland

Ulster

North West

North East

Midlands

Wales

Anglia

South West

LaSER

Channel Islands

Alderney

Guernsey

Hern

Sark

Jersey

Can you imagine how many Guides there are in the UK?

1. Find out how many Guide units there are in your Division.

2. Imagine there's a similar number in all Divisions. How many Divisions are there in your County?

3. How many Counties in your Country or Region?

4. Now if your maths skills are up to the challenge, try and figure out how many Guide units there are in your Country or Region!

In each one of those units there are Guides enjoying similar activities to the ones you do.

Don't forget all the Rainbow units, Brownie Packs and Senior Section groups there are in your Division... your County... your Country or Region... the whole UK...

Tip

Your District or Division Commissioner might be able to provide you with some answers.

Now can you imagine how big your guiding family is? And that's just in this country...

BGIFC...

... stands for British Guides in Foreign Countries. Lots of British girls who live abroad follow the UK guiding programme and meet in Guide units just like yours!

Since 1910, Guiding has grown from a few determined girls wearing Scouts' hats to ten million girls and women in over 140 different countries. WAGGGS was formed in 1928 to link everyone together.

The World Association has its own badge. Any Guide can wear this badge.

Aroundtheworld

All Guides and Girl Scouts, wherever they live, share some things:

- making a Promise
- doing a Good Turn every day
- the World Badge
- the World Flag
- the salute
- the left handshake
- Thinking Day.

Look in *Patrol x-tra* to find out more about the World Badge and what it means.

Wherever you travel in the world you are likely to find Girl Guides or Girl Scouts. More than 5,000 Guides a year travel to meet old friends and make new ones.

There are lots of ways to make international friends...

take part in an international camp in the UK.

... if you're lucky, your unit might go abroad. Why not ask your Leader about this?

isit one of Guiding's World Centres: Pax dge in London, Our Chalet in Switzerland, r Cabaña in Mexico or Sangam in India. e *Patrol x-tra* for more info.

older Guides could travel as art of their Baden-Powell dventure (see page 72).

... as an older Guide you may get the chance to represent Girlguiding UK on a trip abroad. (See *Patrol x-tra* for more information.)

Find out more – ask your Leader about opportunities in your area. You can also check out the WAGGGS website www.wagggsworld.org or the international pages at www.girlguiding.org.uk.

What'sinstore

Crack the code to discover some of the cool things you could experience while you're a Guide! One has been done to start you off.

Tip

It'll help if you fill in the alphabet grid first.

A
B
C
D
E
F
G
H
I
J
K
L
M
N
O
P
Q
R
S
T
U
V
W
X
Y
Z

14 9 1 25 8 24 18 21
T E A M W O R K

11 12 26   13 24   11 24 18   17 14 16
□□□ □□ □□□ □□□

22 1 14 18 24 23 16   22 18 24 25 17 16 9
□□□□□□□ □□□□□□□

5 15 1 23 23 9 26 13 9   5 1 25 22 16
□□□□□□□□□ □□□□□

16 23 9 9 22 24 10 9 18 16   11 18 17 9 26 7 16 15 17 22
□□□□□□□□□□ □□□□□□□□□□

12 26 17 14   13 12 17 7 9 23 17 26 9 16
□□□□ □□□□□□□□□

Now use this code, or make up one of your own, for these other exciting activities!

C O M M U N I T Y   A C T I O N
□□□□□□□□□ □□□□□□

I N T E R N A T I O N A L   T R A V E L
□□□□□□□□□□□□□ □□□□□□

Getting into Guides

There's no end to the new things you can do at Guides. You'll have a great time with your Patrol trying out Go For It! activity packs. You'll have the chance to get active in your community, try exciting challenges, and take your pick from the huge range of interest badges. Then, of course, there's the adventure of going away with your Guide friends. And it all comes together when you earn your Guide Challenge Badges. Read on to find out more!

Once you have joined a Patrol and signed the Unit Guidelines you are officially a Guide! So what happens now? Well, this is where the fun really kicks off.

A Go For It! is a pack full of activities for Patrols to do together. You can use them at any time for activity ideas. Each Go For It! is based on a theme – like hair and beauty, healthy eating or even party planning!

If you spend four Patrol Times on or Go For It!, you have completed it and earned a Go For It! card to keep in your *G file*. You need to have earned two Go For It! cards to gain a Challenge Badge (see page 50).

GoForIt!

There are new Go For Its! being added to the range all the time. Here are some that your unit might have:

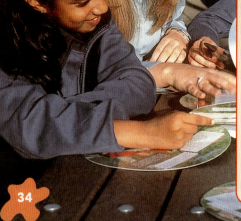

Go For It! Football

Go For It! Peace

Go For It! Chocolate

Go For It! Five senses

Go For It! Communicate

Go For It! I will survive!

Go For It! Healthy eating

Go For It! Be constructive

Go For It! Fitness

Go For It! Blast from the past

Go For It! Life wise

Go For It! On the move

Go For It! With a splash

Go For It! Lights, camera, action!

Go For It! Parties

Go For It! Teamwork

Go For It! Animal active

Go For It! Glamorama!

Your unit will have a selection of Go For Its! for the Patrols to choose from. Some of them are available on the Girlguiding UK website **www.girlguiding.org.uk** for you to download.

Perhaps you and your Patrol have an idea for a Go For It! of your own? Why not create it? Take a look in *Patrol x-tra* for more information.

GoForIt!plans

Go For It!

Patrol time	Date	Activity	What I need to bring/remember

Go For It!

Patrol time	Date	Activity	What I need to bring/remember

Go For It!

Patrol time	Date	Activity	What I need to bring/remember

These charts will help you plan your
part in your Patrol's Go For Its!

Go For It!

Patrol time	Date	Activity	What I need to bring/remember

Go For It!

Patrol time	Date	Activity	What I need to bring/remember

Go For It!

Patrol time	Date	Activity	What I need to bring/remember

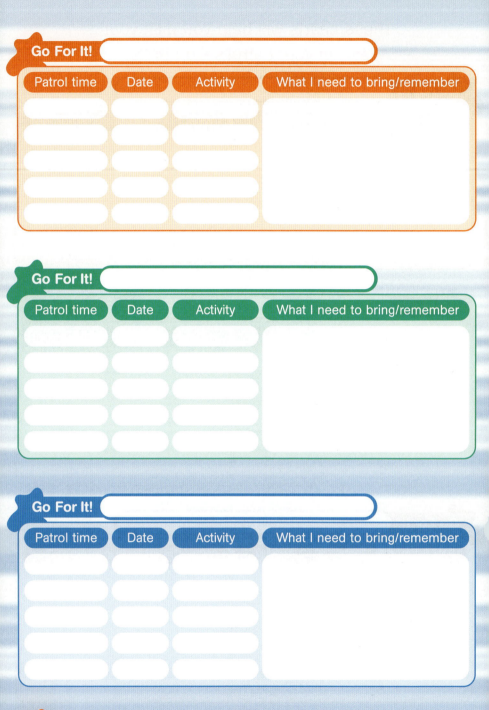

Go For It!

Patrol time	Date	Activity	What I need to bring/remember

Go For It!

Patrol time	Date	Activity	What I need to bring/remember

Go For It!

Patrol time	Date	Activity	What I need to bring/remember

Go For It!

Patrol time	Date	Activity	What I need to bring/remember

Go For It!

Patrol time	Date	Activity	What I need to bring/remember

Go For It!

Patrol time	Date	Activity	What I need to bring/remember

GoForIt!record

You can keep a record of the Go For Its! you have completed here.

Date	Go For It!

Give yourself a sticker each time you complete one!

Guides love the chance to get out of the meeting place and into action – whether it's a quick game of rounders, cooking on a wood fire or going away on holiday.

Outandabout

Keep a note of the things you get up to outside your meeting place.

Date	Activity

Community Action

Community Action is all about helping to make a difference in your community. Your community can mean your neighbourhood, your town, your region, your country, or the whole world. There are lots of different kinds of Community Action and different ways to take part.

Here are some ideas:

- helping at Rainbows or Brownies
- helping at your local place of worship
- taking part in an ICE Project – more details in *Patrol x-tra*
- raising funds for or volunteering with a local or international charity, such as Amnesty International
- recycling cans, bottles, paper etc
- helping out at a charity shop
- reading to people who are blind, elderly or infirm
- volunteering at local events such as carnivals and galas
- cleaning up your environment
- taking action on environmental issues that affect your local community.

You can do Community Action on your own, as a Patrol or as a unit, District, Division or County.

You may have many more ideas – just look around to see where you can make a difference to your community. Talk to your Patrol about Community Action in your area. Make plans, have fun, and make a real difference. Check out *Patrol X-tra* for inspiration too!

Community Action record

Fill in the Community Action activities you have done.

Date	What we did

43

Badges

Doing a badge is a great way of exploring something you're interested in. There are loads to choose from – whatever you're into, there will be a badge for you. You can work towards interest badges on your own, with your Patrol or even as a unit. Each Go For It! has badges linked to it, so if you or your Patrol enjoyed a particular activity as part of a Go For It!, look further and see if there is a badge you can work towards.

You will find syllabuses for all the badges in the Guide *Badge file*. Your Patrol or unit may have a copy of the *Badge file* that you can browse through.

Badge file

If you are interested in working for a badge, check the syllabus and speak to your Leader about your plans.

Badgerecord

Challenge Badges

Challenge Badges bring all the different bits of guiding together and celebrate what you have achieved. You do your Challenge Badges as an individual. Each one takes 12 months to complete.

There are four Challenge Badges, each a different colour.

1st Challenge Badge — blue

2nd Challenge Badge — pink

3rd Challenge Badge — purple

4th Challenge Badge — gold

Look at page 49 to see what you need to do for a Challenge Badge. Then you can use the record pages from page 50 onwards to fill in what you do and when you do it.

GuideChallengeBadge

This shows your commitment to guiding and takes 12 months to complete.

1 Over a 12-month period, be a reliable member of your Patrol. Talk to your Patrol about what it is like to belong to that team and make one suggestion for improvement. Sign and keep the unit's Guidelines. If you have sometimes found the Guidelines difficult to keep, discuss this with your Patrol and make suggestions for changes.

2 Complete at least two Go For Its! with your Patrol and help to decide what you do. If you have used a Go For It! successfully for four Patrol times, the Go For It! is completed.

3 Complete two activities outside your meeting place.

4 Take part in a community activity that involves doing something for somebody else. This should be different from your activities in clause 3.

5 Share with your Patrol your favourite guiding experiences over the past 12 months. If possible have a look at the Guide pages on the Girlguiding UK web site (www.girlguiding.org.uk) to see what is happening at a UK level.

1stChallengeBadge

I am a member of _____ Patrol

The other members of my Patrol are:

(PL)

(PS)

I have signed the Unit Guidelines

I have been a reliable and responsible member of my Patrol in these ways:

I completed these Go For Its!:

Go For It!	Date

I joined in these activities away from our usual meeting place:

Date	
Where we went:	
What we did:	
Date	
Where we went:	
What we did:	

I completed this Community Action activity:

Date	
Activity	
Who I did this activity with:	
How it helped:	

My favourite guiding experience over the past 12 months was:

I told my Patrol about this on:

I was awarded my 1st Challenge Badge on:

2nd Challenge Badge

I am a member of _____ Patrol

The other members of my Patrol are:

(PL) _____

(PS) _____

_____

_____

_____

_____

_____

I have signed the Unit Guidelines ⬭

I have been a reliable and responsible member of my Patrol in these ways:

I completed these Go For Its!:

Go For It!	Date

I joined in these activities away from our usual meeting place:

Date	
Where we went:	
What we did:	

Date	
Where we went:	
What we did:	

I completed this Community Action activity:

Date	
Activity	
Who I did this activity with:	
How it helped:	

My favourite guiding experience over the past 12 months was:

I told my Patrol about this on:

I was awarded my 2nd Challenge Badge on:

3rdChallengeBadge

I am a member of _____ Patrol

The other members of my Patrol are:

(PL) _____

(PS) _____

_____

_____

_____

_____

_____

I have signed the Unit Guidelines ⬤

I have been a reliable and responsible member of my Patrol in these ways:

I completed these Go For Its!:

Go For It!	Date

I joined in these activities away from our usual meeting place:

Date	
Where we went:	
What we did:	

Date	
Where we went:	
What we did:	

I completed this Community Action activity:

Date	
Activity	
Who I did this activity with:	
How it helped:	

My favourite guiding experience over the past 12 months was:

I told my Patrol about this on:

I was awarded my 3rd Challenge Badge on:

4thChallengeBadge

I am a member of _____ Patrol

The other members of my Patrol are:

(PL)

(PS)

I have signed the Unit Guidelines

I have been a reliable and responsible member of my Patrol in these ways:

I completed these Go For Its!:

Go For It!	Date

I joined in these activities away from our usual meeting place:

Date	
Where we went:	
What we did:	

Date	
Where we went:	
What we did:	

I completed this Community Action activity:

Date	
Activity	
Who I did this activity with:	
How it helped:	

My favourite guiding experience over the past 12 months was:

I told my Patrol about this on:

I was awarded my 4th Challenge Badge on:

Challengingtimes

Name of Challenge	
What I did	
Who did it with me	
When I finished it	
How I rated it	

Name of Challenge	
What I did	
Who did it with me	
When I finished it	
How I rated it	

Sometimes special, one-off Challenges are set by your Division, County, Region, or Girlguiding UK. Use these pages to record any that you complete in your time as a Guide.

Name of Challenge	
What I did	
Who did it with me	
When I finished it	
How I rated it	

Name of Challenge	
What I did	
Who did it with me	
When I finished it	
How I rated it	

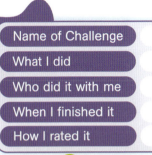

You can choose to use two of these Challenges as clauses for your Baden-Powell Challenge – as long as you completed the special Challenge after you began to work on the Baden Powell Challenge (see page 71).

Campsand holidays

Ask any Guide what is the very best thing about Guides – chances are she will say 'going away'! Whether you go on a camp, a holiday or a sleepover, there are lots of different opportunities and they are all fantastic fun.

Camps

As a Guide you might camp with your unit, District, Division or County. You could go away for one night, a weekend or a whole week. If any of you holds a Guide Camp Permit (see page 65) you can even camp just as a Patrol. Camps can be large or small, but the one thing they all have in common is that they are a great adventure. You'll live with your friends in tents, in the great outdoors, cook your own food and join in some fun outdoor activities. Camping is an ideal opportunity to learn about the outdoors: you could try survival skills, lighting fires, sleeping under the stars, going walking, playing wide games (games played over a large area), orienteering, pioneering, water sports or lots of other activities.

Holidays

Guide holidays are just as much fun as camps. You stay indoors in youth hostels, village halls or guiding centres. You'll have a great time with your friends, doing your own cooking and all sorts of activities that you choose. A camp or holiday may be on a theme that you've chosen, such as 'Sports', 'The Circus' or a favourite film.

Overnights

These last only one night and take place in Guide halls, youth hostels, at camp or even at museums or Sea Life Centres. An overnight means you can visit places that are too far to go to in a day, and have extra fun with your Guide friends.

Sleepovers

These are for Patrols – no Leaders! – and take place in a Patrol member's home, with the permission of their parents, your parents and Leader. It may only be overnight, but sleepovers help you to get to know your Patrol better and do those activities that you can't always fit into your Guide meetings.

International travel

Once you've been away with Guides and found out how much you love it, you can be more adventurous and try camping or holidaying abroad. Your unit might travel abroad together to an international jamboree or one of Guiding's World Centres.

Don't worry if your unit doesn't go abroad, as there are lots of international opportunities available each year for individuals – ask your Leader for details. If you want to represent Girlguiding UK at an event abroad, you may need to attend an international opportunities weekend with lots of other Guides. Even if you are not chosen to attend an event, these weekends are a great experience on their own.

Kitlist

When you go away with Guides, you'll need to take the right stuff! Your Leader will give you a kit list for each camp or holiday. You can also use this list to tick things off as you pack them. There are enough tick boxes for several camps or holidays.

Put name labels on your stuff so you don't lose it!

Keeping clean

Towels (2 small ones, not one large)

Wash bag

Flannel

Soap/shower gel

Toothbrush/paste

Shampoo

Deodorant

Hairbrush/bands

Tampons/towels

Tissues

Eating

Drawstring bag containing:

Two plates

Bowl

Mug

Cutlery

Tea towel

Sleeping

Sleeping bag

Pillow and case

Groundsheet

Camping mat

Clothes

Cagoule and overtrousers	Hat
Underwear	Socks
Jacket or fleece	Swimsuit
Nightclothes	T-shirts
Indoor shoes	Wellies
Jumpers	Shorts
Trousers (not jeans if possible)	Trainers / walking shoes

Other stuff

Notebook and pens	Magazine or book
Torch and batteries	Camera and film
Alarm clock	Empty drinks bottle
Stamps	*G file*
Cash and a purse	Spare glasses/lenses

Depending on the weather

Woolly hat, scarf and gloves

Hat, sunglasses, sun cream, insect repellant

If you're camping, a rucksack or holdall is easier than a suitcase. Keep your bedding dry in a holdall or similar, lined with a plastic bag.

Camp/ holidayrecord

You can keep a record of your residential events here.

Give each event a score out of ten.

Date	Where we went	No. of nights	Tent/indoors	Score

CampPermit

When you're an experienced camper you might like to start taking more responsibility for organising camps. Gaining your Camp Permit means you'll be able to run a camp with just other Guides – no Leader!

When can I start working towards the Camp Permit?

- You need to be at least 12 years old and to have gained the Camper Advanced badge.
- Your Leader, Patrol Leaders' Council or Guides you work with need to agree that you're ready.

How do I gain the Camp Permit?

Organise and run a camp for two or three nights.

Who can go on a Guide Permit Camp?

- Yourself plus three to five Guides (or up to seven if two of them have camped before).
- You can take your own Patrol or you can form a Patrol just for this camp.

Who will help me with the camp?

- Your Leader.
- Your Patrol.
- An adult who will be close by if needed during your camp (this may be your Unit Leader).
- An experienced Guider, called a Mentor, who will look at your plans, offer advice and visit you at camp. She will sign your modules when they are completed (see pages 67–70). She should not be your Unit Leader.

What do I need to do?

With the help of your Leader you:

- Find an approved venue.
- Work out the cost of the camp and complete simple records of money spent.
- Distribute and collect the necessary Girlguiding UK forms.
- Find an adult to be close by during the camp.

With your Patrol:

- Plan a programme of activities, taking into account everyone's needs.
- Plan a menu and how you will cook your food.
- Work out how to get everyone and the equipment to and from camp.
- Agree camp guidelines, and share out the jobs for camp.

Your responsibilities are:

- Making a plan of your campsite to show where everything should go.
- Seeing that all the equipment is looked after, including tents, bedding, first aid, kitchen and cooking equipment.
- Being responsible for camp hygiene and the Patrol's safety.
- Displaying your programme plan, menus and rotas.
- Making sure you have all the equipment for activities and have booked any instructors needed.
- Having alternative activities ready in case you have to change your plans.
- Collecting camp fees and paying the camp expenses.
- Collecting the necessary forms, keeping them safe during camp and giving them to your Leader after camp.
- Tidying up after camp. Remember that: 'A Guide leaves nothing but her thanks.'

Modules

Module 1: Plan a residential event

		Mentor's signature	Guide's signature
Element 1a	With your Patrol, decide on the type of event.		
Element 1b	Choose where you are going to stay.		
Element 1c	With your Leader, find an adult to act as emergency support.		

Module 2: Plan the camp

		Mentor's signature	Guide's signature
Element 2a	Look after the money side of the camp.		
Element 2b	Decide on equipment needed.		
Element 2c	Complete necessary Girlguiding UK forms.		
Element 2d	Plan what you have to do at the end of the camp.		

Module 3: Plan to be safe

		Mentor's signature	Guide's signature
Element 3a	Plan for emergencies.		
Element 3b	Agree event guidelines with your Patrol.		

Module 4: Plan your food and how you will cook it

		Mentor's signature	Guide's signature
Element 4a	Plan cooking and storage facilities.		
Element 4b	With your Patrol, plan your menus.		
Element 4c	Understand the importance of food hygiene and waste disposal.		

Module 5: Make health and first aid arrangements

		Mentor's signature	Guide's signature
Element 5a	Find out about the site's showers, toilets and water supply.		
Element 5b	Be prepared for any possible emergency.		
Element 5c	Check the first aid kit.		

Module 6: Find the activity equipment you need

		Mentor's signature	Guide's signature
Element 6a	Check the condition of equipment.		
Element 6b	Make sure everyone knows how to use the equipment.		
Element 6c	Return/replace used equipment.		

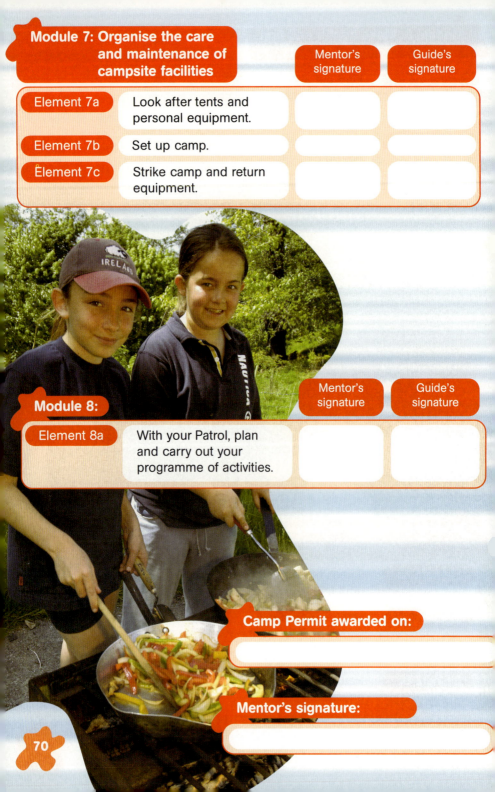

Module 7: Organise the care and maintenance of campsite facilities

		Mentor's signature	Guide's signature
Element 7a	Look after tents and personal equipment.		
Element 7b	Set up camp.		
Element 7c	Strike camp and return equipment.		

Module 8:

		Mentor's signature	Guide's signature
Element 8a	With your Patrol, plan and carry out your programme of activities.		

Camp Permit awarded on:

Mentor's signature:

70

Reach for theskies:
TheBaden-Powell Challenge

Are you up for excitement, challenge and adventure? Do you want to gain the highest award a Guide can achieve? Read on to find out all about the Baden-Powell Challenge Award.

Planning your Challenge

To start the Baden-Powell Challenge you need to have:

- made your Promise
- gained at least two Guide Challenge Badges
- gained at least two interest badges.

This shows your commitment to guiding.

The Baden-Powell Challenge is divided into five zones, each containing lots of different clauses (see pages 74–88). You need to complete ten clauses in total. You should do one from each zone, then five more. These can come from any of the zones. Up to two of them can relate to Country/Region or Girlguiding UK initiatives (see page 58).

To finish the Award, you need to take part in a Baden-Powell Adventure. These are usually residential events organised by your County or Country/Region for all Guides in the area who are doing the Baden-Powell Challenge. The Adventure is all about celebrating what you have achieved, trying something new and meeting other Guides who have been doing similar things. Dates of Baden-Powell Adventures are advertised in Country/Region and County newsletters, and in *Guiding magazine*.

When you have finished eight clauses, fill in the fold-out notification form (it's at the end of your *G file*) and ask your Leader to sign it. She will give you contact details for the person who will organise your Adventure. They will then get in touch with you to discuss it.

When you are ready to go for your Baden-Powell Challenge, discuss with your Leader:

1 **Your personal plan**

- What you have chosen from each zone. Make sure each clause is a personal challenge to you.
- Over what time period you will do the Challenge.

2 **Your support plan**
- What help you will need from your Patrol and unit.
- What help you will need from your Leader.
- What help you will need from your family.

Use the spaces on the following pages to plan and record your Challenge.

When you've completed all the clauses and taken part in your Adventure, you should arrange to meet your District Commissioner. She will be pleased to know that you have completed the Baden-Powell Challenge. She'll want to find out what you did and how you feel your understanding of the Promise will help you in the future.

Challenge syllabus

Zone 1: Healthy lifestyles

Aim: To encourage Guides to lead a healthy lifestyle by promoting physical, emotional and spiritual well-being.

1 Organise and run a Patrol cooking competition. You could provide ingredients and challenge the Patrols to produce dishes in a set time.

2 Set yourself three personal fitness goals and keep a diary for a month to show how you have worked towards them.

3 Run an activity session for your Patrol on an issue which concerns young people today.

Find out about 4ward, 4self, 4others (a peer education initiative). See page 109 for more!

74

4 Help to organise a sports competition with another Patrol or another Guide unit, eg mini-Olympics, fitness trail or team games evening.

5 Complete one of the following badges: Agility, Cook, Healthy Lifestyles, Sports.

7 Organise a sponsored fitness event for a good cause.

6 With your Patrol, plan and carry out a 'Reflections' session around a chosen theme. You could include a relaxation or meditation aspect or use mime, readings, music, dance or slides.

8 Produce a cookbook of healthy recipes appropriate for Rainbows, Brownies or Guides to use at an event, holiday or camp.

Zone1:Healthylifestyles

Clause number

What I will do and why

What help I will need

Who I will do it with

How long it will take

Date it was completed

Zone2: Globalawareness

Aim: To increase awareness of global issues and of the contribution each Guide can make.

1 Find out about the life a child from a country in the global south (the developing world) leads. Share your findings with your Patrol.

2 Organise an activity for your Patrol or unit which will help somebody from a country in the global south (the developing world). Let your local International Adviser know what you are doing.

3 Complete one of the following badges: Interpreter, World Cultures, World Guiding, World Issues, World Traveller.

4 With your Patrol, organise an international evening with games, crafts, food or music and dance.

5 Design a poster on a current global issue and use it to make a presentation to your unit.

6 Use the Internet or your local library to find out about fair trade. Survey what fair trade items are available in your area, for example in your local supermarket. Organise an activity about fair trade with your Patrol.

7 Find out about the Guide Friendship Fund and hold a fund-raising evening to support its work.

Zone2:Globalawareness

Clause number

What I will do and why

What help I will need

Who I will do it with

How long it will take

Date it was completed

79

Zone3: Discovery

Aim: To challenge Guides with new experiences and adventure.

1 Make a bivouac and spend the night in it. Make your own breakfast the following morning.

2 Start a new hobby or craft, or extend an existing one, and work on it for at least three months. You could try glass painting, learning a musical instrument, football, candle making, rollerblading or stargazing. Find out about your hobby's origins, history and rules. Do a presentation on your hobby for your Patrol in a way that is new to you.

3 Attend a residential event somewhere new to you, eg in a youth hostel or on a narrowboat. Your Baden-Powell Adventure cannot count for this clause.

4 Complete the Outdoor Pursuits badge.

5 Visit a city farm, rescue centre or nature reserve. Discuss with your Patrol why it is important to have these and who benefits from them. What could you do to help?

6 With friends, attend an event such as the theatre, ballet, an open air concert or a pop concert. Record your thoughts and impressions and share them with your Young Leader or Leader.

Stay safe when you are out and about.

7 Use ICT skills to make a new resource for your unit. What about making a 'Welcome to Guides' pack, a 'Guide to camp' or a songbook? You could use photography, video, computers etc.

8 Complete the Guide Camp Permit.

Zone3:Discovery

Clause number

What I will do and why

What help I will need

Who I will do it with

How long it will take

Date it was complet

Zone4:
Skillsandrelationships

Aim: To develop Guides' self-confidence and self-worth and to improve their interpersonal and life skills.

1 Organise a party for someone outside your unit, such as your local Brownies, your family, or girls not normally involved in guiding; or hold a bring-a-friend party at Guides.

2 Organise a cooperative games evening for your unit, such as parachute games.

Look in *Patrol x-tra* for ideas!

3 Help organise a trip with your Patrol to see something of interest to you. Go on the trip and report back to your unit.

4 Find out what there is available for young people in your area. With your unit, organise a discussion to find out about local issues which affect you and what young people can do to assist.

Check out your local Connexions centre or speak to a local councillor.

5 Complete one of the following badges: Communicator, Independent Living, Personal Safety, Water Safety.

6 Organise an activity based on today's clothing. You could do an analysis of what is suitable for certain activities, what's currently fashionable and what makes you feel good. Present your findings in an interesting way.

7 Raise money to take part in your Baden-Powell Adventure. Could anyone else benefit from your fund-raising?

8 Complete the Active Response or First Aid badge. Hold a First Aid evening for your unit, including incidents and fake wounds, to demonstrate your new skills.

Zone4:Skillsandrelationships

Clause number

What I will do and why

What help I will need

Who I will do it with

How long it will take

Date it was completed

Zone5: Celebratingdiversity

Aim: To promote active citizenship among Guides, developing their awareness of rights and responsibilities for all.

1 With your Patrol or unit, celebrate a festival from a culture other than your own, eg Diwali, harvest festival, Chinese New Year, Thai Festival of Lights.

2 Organise a disability awareness activity evening or invite someone to your unit to talk about disabilities.

3 Find out about the UN Convention on the Rights of the Child. Organise an activity to share what you have found out.

4 Complete one of these badges: Culture, Discovering Faith, Community Action.

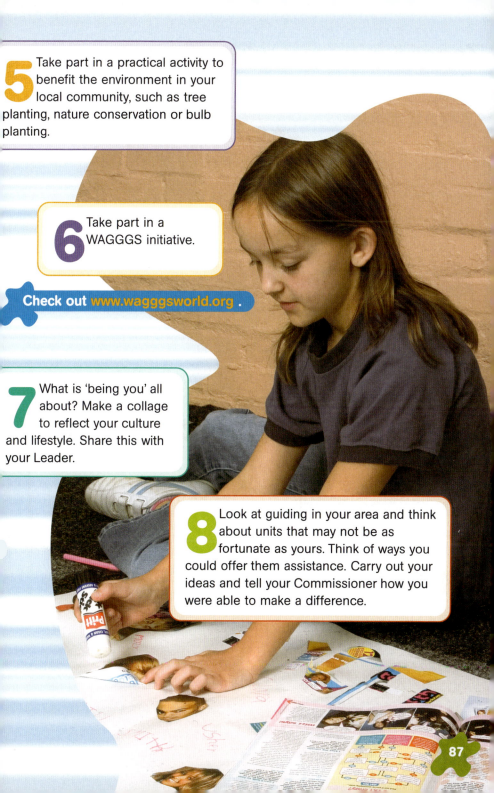

5 Take part in a practical activity to benefit the environment in your local community, such as tree planting, nature conservation or bulb planting.

6 Take part in a WAGGGS initiative.

Check out www.wagggsworld.org .

7 What is 'being you' all about? Make a collage to reflect your culture and lifestyle. Share this with your Leader.

8 Look at guiding in your area and think about units that may not be as fortunate as yours. Think of ways you could offer them assistance. Carry out your ideas and tell your Commissioner how you were able to make a difference.

Zone5:Celebratingdiversity

Clause number

What I will do and why

What help I will need

Who I will do it with

How long it will take

Date it was completed

Keep track of your five additional clauses here.

Zone and clause

What I will do and why

What help I will need

Who I will do it with

How long it will take

Date it was completed

Zone and clause

What I will do and why

What help I will need

Who I will do it with

How long it will take

Date it was completed

Zone and clause

What I will do and why

What help I will need

Who I will do it with

How long it will take

Date it was completed

Zone and clause

What I will do and why

What help I will need

Who I will do it with

How long it will take

Date it was complete

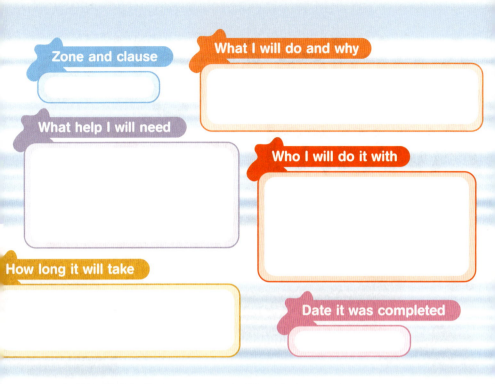

Zone and clause

What I will do and why

What help I will need

Who I will do it with

How long it will take

Date it was completed

Adventure

After completing all ten clauses, you should attend a Baden-Powell Adventure. Record your experience here.

Where I went

When I went

Who I went with/met

Highlight(s) of my Adventure

Achieving the Award

Baden-Powell Adventure organiser's signature

I met my Commissioner on

Commissioner's signature

My Baden-Powell Challenge Badge was awarded on

Lifesupport

We all have times when things are not going so well. The most important thing is not to struggle on alone – there's always someone who could help. On the next few pages you'll find advice and ideas for dealing with all kinds of difficult situations.

Knowing how to take control and get help is always useful. You might be able to help your friends as well as yourself.

Bullying

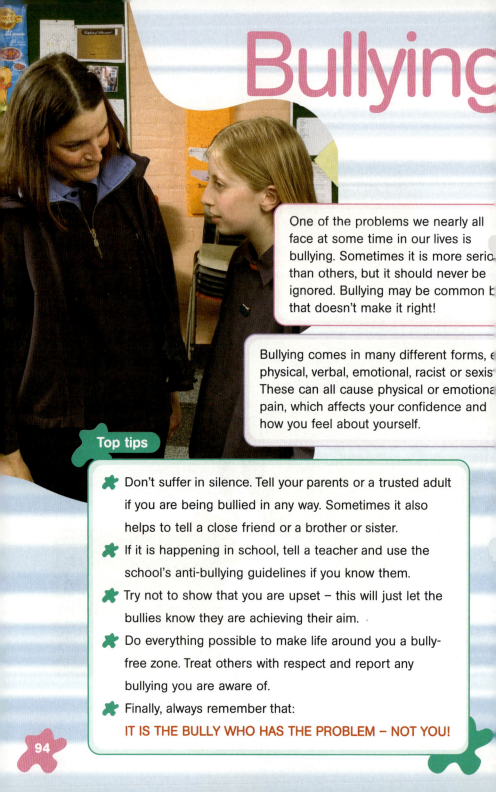

One of the problems we nearly all face at some time in our lives is bullying. Sometimes it is more serio than others, but it should never be ignored. Bullying may be common b that doesn't make it right!

Bullying comes in many different forms, e physical, verbal, emotional, racist or sexis These can all cause physical or emotiona pain, which affects your confidence and how you feel about yourself.

Top tips

⭐ Don't suffer in silence. Tell your parents or a trusted adult if you are being bullied in any way. Sometimes it also helps to tell a close friend or a brother or sister.

⭐ If it is happening in school, tell a teacher and use the school's anti-bullying guidelines if you know them.

⭐ Try not to show that you are upset – this will just let the bullies know they are achieving their aim.

⭐ Do everything possible to make life around you a bully-free zone. Treat others with respect and report any bullying you are aware of.

⭐ Finally, always remember that:

IT IS THE BULLY WHO HAS THE PROBLEM – NOT YOU!

Is there anything in your Unit Guidelines about bullying? If not, do you think there should be? Write a guideline that you feel would help to stamp out bullying.

The Anti Bullying Campaign has a helpline you can call for counselling and advice about bullying: 020 7378 1446. These websites might also be useful:

- www.antibullying.net
- www.dfes.gov.uk/bullying
- www.need2know.co.uk

Findinghelp

When life gets tough it's tempting to believe that no one can understand how you feel, or do anything to help. But take heart – there is a lot of help and advice out there. You can always talk to your Guide Leaders in confidence. They have lots of experience of working with young people, and will be happy to talk to you.

There might be issues you think are really important, or you would like to understand more about. Guides is an ideal place to explore the things that affect you – whether that's healthy eating, smoking or exam stress. Your Patrol or unit can all support one another. And it doesn't all have to be heavy stuff – you can deal with some things in a fun way too!

General

Childline: 0800 1111
The website **www.childline.org.uk** has advice on many issues, like exam stress, friendships and health.
NSPCC Child Protection Helpline: 0800 800 500
Careline: 020 8514 1177
Offers counselling and advice on any subject.
The Samaritans: 0845 7 90 90 90
Or email: jo@samaritans.org
Youth 2 Youth: 020 8896 3675
Support and advice for young people.

Smoking and alcohol

ASH: **www.ash.org.uk**
Information on all aspects of smoking and the tobacco industry.
Alateen: 020 7403 0888
Advice for teens with alcohol concerns.
National Association for Children of Alcoholics: 0800 567123

97

Eating Disorders Association: 01603 621414
National Phobics Society: 0161 227 9898
Cruse Bereavement Care Young Person's Helpline: 0808 808 1677
Offers counselling after the death of someone close.
Get Connected: 0800 096 0096
For young people who have run away or are thinking of doing so.
DIAL: 01302 310123
Disability information.
youngGov: http://younggov.ukonline.gov.uk
Makes government information accessible to young people.

Overtoyou

**If you find any more useful
numbers or sites, add them here:**

Emergencies

An emergency is any dangerous incident that happens suddenly and needs quick action to remove or reduce the danger. At Guides you'll have plenty of chances to learn about good ways to deal with emergencies. For example, you could take your First Aid, Active Response, Fire Safety or Water Safety badge (see the *Badge file* to find out more).

If you ever need to take charge in an emergency, you'll need to do several things at once. This simple plan will help you deal with the incident in the best possible way.

Assess the situation:

* Find out what has happened.
* Ask if anyone else can help.

Safety

* Don't do anything unless you're sure it is safe. You won't be able to help if you get hurt too.
* If you can, tell an adult as soon as possible.

Call the emergency services: dial **999** and give them as much detail as possible (see opposite).

Remember

Try to stay calm. This will reassure everybody, especially the casualty.

Don't try and give first aid unless you have been trained. Do not move the casualty. Just keep her warm and tell her she will be OK and that help is on the way.

If you've done your best, that's all anyone can ask of you. If you have any worries afterwards, talk them over with your parents or a trusted adult.

Calling the emergency services:

You can contact the emergency services from any phone.
You don't need to pay: just dial 999.
When you dial, the operator will ask you which emergency service you want:

- police
- ambulance
- fire service
- coastguard
- mine, mountain, cave and fell rescue.

Ask for the service you need, and tell the operator the telephone number you are calling from and your name.

When you have been put through to the correct service you will be asked for these details:

- the telephone number you are calling from (if you are on a mobile they may not need to ask you this)
- where the incident is
- the type of incident
- anything you know about the casualties, eg how many, what is wrong with them. You can also warn the emergency service of any dangers, such as ice or leaking petrol.

You will be told when you can put the phone down.

Be prepared

Getting some first aid training will help you feel more confident about dealing with an emergency. You could:

- Complete the Guide First Aid badge.
- Contact St John Ambulance, The British Red Cross or St Andrew's Ambulance to find out about any courses they run. You can write their contact details here:

As a Guide, you'll take part in all sorts of exciting activities which have been carefully checked so that they are safe as well as enjoyable. Your Leaders have been trained to lead or supervise the activities so that everything is as safe as possible.

Stayingsafe

However, you also need to take some responsibility for your own safety, both at Guides and in your everyday life. Taking these steps will help you keep safe at all times.

Safety tips

🌸 Let friends and family know where you are going, who with, how you are getting there and when you expect to be back. If you are delayed, phone to let them know.

🌸 Always keep to the route that you have told your friends and family you will be following. Do not use remote, lonely or badly lit streets.

🌸 Try to walk home in a group – or ask someone to collect you.

🌸 Keep your money, jewellery, mobile phone or other valuables out of sight.

🌸 If you think you are being followed, keep moving towards the nearest public place, eg a shop, café or police station, so you can tell an adult or phone home.

🌸 Have your keys ready so you can get indoors quickly.

🌸 If someone tries to snatch your belongings – give them up. They can be replaced and it isn't worth risking getting hurt.

🌸 Be aware of traffic and listen for people approaching. It's not a good idea to listen to a personal stereo.

🌸 Walk facing oncoming traffic, so you can see what's coming and so that cars cannot crawl behind or beside you.

🌸 If someone asks for directions, don't get too close, especially to people in cars. **Never** get into a car to show someone the way.

🌸 If you are travelling alone by bus, train or Tube, always try to sit in a busy area. Note where the alarms are on trains. On buses, sit near the driver.

🌸 If you see something suspicious or think that someone has tried to harm you, phone 999 and talk to the police.

If you feel threatened, trust your instincts and take some action!

-  Make some noise to attract attention and confuse your attacker.
- Shout instructions like 'Phone the police!'
- Run if necessary.
- Attract the driver's or conductor's attention if you are on public transport.
- Tell your parents or a trusted adult at once, giving them as much detail as possible.

Lifeskills

Guides is a great place to learn new skills – and you can use them in everyday life too! Think of some things you have learned at Guides and how they will help you at home, at school or at social events.

Skills learned at Guides

Skill	How/when it will help me
Learning to work as a Patrol	Working in teams for school projects

In the same way, things you learn outside Guides will help you at unit meetings, camps etc.

Skills learned outside Guides

Skill	How I can use it at Guides
Computer skills	Use for *GFI! Communicate* or to write the unit newsletter

What'snext?

By now you're probably enjoying Guides so much, you never want to leave. But don't worry – there is life after Guides!

You'll find even more fun, friends and new experiences in the Senior Section. It's for members aged between 14 and 25, and there are loads of different things you can do. Rangers, Young Leaders and In4mers are all Senior Section members. As you get older, more opportunities open up – you could be a SSAGO member or a young Guider. Take a look at the options on the next few pages and see which ones will suit you best. If loads of them look great, don't worry – you can do more than one thing at a time!

Moving on to the Senior Section doesn't mean giving up everything you enjoy at Guides. You can still do the same fun things, but with lots of added extras too!

Wanted...

Wanted...

20,000+ Senior Section members seek individuals aged 14–25 for fun and friendship.

Lead the way (14–18)

Enthusiastic, up-for-it Young Leaders wanted for fun times volunteering with young people. Must like Rainbows, Brownies or Guides and be available for weekly meetings. Opportunities include running activities and managing unit finances, as well as going away with your chosen unit. Chance to work on the leadership qualification Making It Count!, and on the adult Leadership Qualification once you are 16. YL groups meet in some areas. GSOH a must!

GROUP DYNAMICS (14+)

Rangers and other Senior Section groups provide you with opportunities and challenges that are created just for you! The Look Wider programme is packed full of ideas, but most groups include activities from many other sources as well. Some groups specialise in particular awards or activities – look out for Duke of Edinburgh's Award groups, for example. Remember, in the Senior Section it's your programme, and you decide what you want to do!

Fancy a challenge? (16+)

Want to do something different? The Queen's Guide Award is the highest award in guiding. It's an exciting challenge that anyone aged 16 or over can work for. It has five clauses: Service in Guiding, Outdoor Challenge, Personal Skill Development, Community Action and Residential Experience. Go on – surprise yourself!

Go 4 it (14+)

4ward, 4 self, 4 others is a peer education initiative for Senior Section members. It's a chance to learn about new topics and gain the skills to inform and educate your peers, inside and outside guiding. When you've completed a basic training you'll be called an In4mer, and you can put your skills into practice by running sessions or just chatting informally with your peers!

OPEN YOUR EYES (14+)

Look Wider is the programme for the Senior Section. It is based on eight areas such as Personal values, Creativity and Fit for life. You can choose what activities you want to do and when you want to do them. All Senior Section members can work on Look Wider.

Have your say (16+)

Once you're 16 you can take part in Innovate, Girlguiding UK's Youth Forum, where Senior Section members from all over the country get together to shape the future of Girlguiding UK. Many Regions and Counties also have Youth Forums where Senior Section members can have their say at a local level. Then there's the British Youth Council, where Girlguiding UK's representatives help to influence the government about issues that affect young people. If you have an opinion, this is how you make it count!

Duke of Edinburgh's Award (14+)

Learn new skills, work on rewarding community action, test your physical fitness and take off on an exciting expedition with your friends. Check out **www.theaward.org** for more information. Girlguiding UK gives you the chance to complete the whole award with us, or you can put your guiding experiences towards the award which you might be doing through another organisation, such as school.

Into sport?

The Community Sports Leader Award could be for you. It's a nationally recognised qualification that enables you to plan and run sports programmes in your local community.

Calling all travellers!

Team members needed for exploration and discovery. Must be enthusiastic, interested in other cultures and willing to discuss global issues. Opportunities include travelling with your Senior Section or Ranger unit, as well as GOLD (Guiding Overseas Linked with Development) for those aged 18–30.

Take charge!
(16+)

From the age of 16 you can work towards your Adult Leadership Qualification, either as a Young Leader (if you're under 18) or as a Young Guider (over 18). Young Guiders are part of the Senior Section too, which means you still have all your Senior Section opportunities – but you get all the adult Leader choices too!

Lots in Common (13+)

Go global with the Commonwealth Award. Open to older Guides and Senior Section members in all Commonwealth countries, the award is a great way to find out more about Guiding and international issues and cultures.

SSAGO

... stands for Student Scout And Guide Organisation. It is a good way for students at university or college to stay involved in Guiding and Scouting even if they are not able to attend their regular unit meetings. There are many groups all over the country which organise their own activities. Check your college or university's clubs and societies directory for local contacts.

Stay in touch

The Trefoil Guild is a good way for you to stay in touch with guiding at times when you can't make a regular commitment.

Find out more:

- Ask your Leader for the contact details of your nearest Ranger and Young Leader Guiders.
- Check out **www.girlguiding.org.uk/seniorsection** .
- Invite Senior Section members to a unit meeting, camp or holiday.
- Ask an In4mer to run a session on a hot topic in your Patrol.

Answers:
'What's in store?'

A	1
B	3
C	5
D	7
E	9
F	11
G	13
H	15
I	17
J	19
K	21
L	23
M	25
N	26
O	24
P	22
Q	20
R	18
S	16
T	14
U	12
V	10
W	8
X	6
Y	4
Z	2

Fun   Go   For   Its!
Patrols   Promise
Challenge   Camps
Sleepovers   Friendship
Unit   Guidelines

If you used the same code for the other puzzles, you should have got these answers:

```
C   O   M   M   U   N   I   T   Y        A   C   T   I   O   N
5  24  25  25  12  26  17  14   4        1   5  14  17  24  26

I   N   T   E   R   N   A   T   I   O   N   A   L
17  26  14   9  18  26   1  14  17  24  26   1  23

O   P   P   O   R   T   U   N   I   T   I   E   S
24  22  22  24  18  14  12  26  17  14  17   9  16
```

Stayingin touch

The best thing about Guides is the people you meet. You'll make loads of friends and meet people who can help you as you move on in guiding.

The next few pages can be used as a guiding address book for all your new contacts.

Useful contacts

Use these pages to fill in useful names and addresses. Your Leader should be able to help you with some of the information.

Here are a few to start you off:

Name:	Girlguiding UK's website
Address:	www.girlguiding.org.uk
What's it for:	The latest facts and fun – international, pen pal link, Go For It! news, badge news and so on.

Name:	Country/Region Headquarters
Address:	
What's it for:	

Name:	Local Guide Shop/Depot
Address:	
What's it for:	

Name:

Address:

What's it for:

Name:

Address:

What's it for:

Name:

Address:

What's it for:

Name:

Address:

What's it for:

115

Guidefriends

Going to large scale camps and events is great fun, and you are guaranteed to make new friends. Don't lose touch – swap addresses and you might have found a pen pal for life!

Name:

Address/email:

Where we met:

Name:

Address/email:

Where we met:

Name:

Address/email:

Where we met:

Name:

Address/email:

Where we met:

Name:

Address/email:

Where we met:

Name:

Address/email:

Where we met:

Name:

Address/email:

Where we met:

Name:

Address/email:

Where we met:

Notepages

Baden-Powell Challenge

Notification of near completion

When you have completed eight clauses of your Baden-Powell Challlenge, fill out this form and ask your Leader to sign it. Then send it to the person responsible for organising Baden-Powell Adventures in your area.

Guide's full name:	
Address:	
Date of birth:	
Contact number:	
Email address:	
Unit:	
District:	
Division:	

Promise made on:

Challenge Badges received on:

Interest Badges completed on:

Please list any special interests:

Please list any special dietary, cultural or mobility requirements:

I confirm that _____ (name of Guide) has completed/almost completed the required ten clauses of the Baden-Powell Challenge.

Signed:

(Leader)

Print name:

Date:

What do Guides do? What sort of fun will we have? How many Guides are there? What shall I wear? What will we do at meetings? What badges can I take?

So many questions – and you'll find all the answers here in your *G file!* It's the essential guide to Guides, with all the info you need. Plus there's plenty more:

- lots of pages to fill in
- great stickers
- pockets to keep your badges and certificates safe.

It's all here – so check it out and really get into Guides!

Name